Disadvantage, Politics and Disorder

Social Disintegration and Conflict in Contemporary Britain

John Benyon

Studies in Crime, Order and Policing
Occasional Paper No 1

Series Editor: Roger Matthews

Centre for the Study of Public Order
University of Leicester

STUDIES IN CRIME, ORDER AND POLICING

Research Papers

No 1   M. Gill, with Mary Salmon and Julie Hill, *Crime on Holiday: Abuse, Damage and Theft in Small Holiday Accommodation Units*

No 2   B. Loveday, *Civilian Staff in the Police Force: Competences and Conflicts in the Police Force*

Occasional Papers

No 1   J. Benyon, *Disadvantage, Politics and Disorder: Social Disintegration and Conflict in Contemporary Britain*

No 2   S. Johnson, *Realising the Public World Order: The Growth of United Nations Jurisdiction and Sovereignty*

First Published 1993

Centre for the Study of Public Order, University of Leicester, The Friars, 154 Upper New Walk, Leicester, LE1 7QA

Telephone 0533 522489
Fax 0533 523944

ISBN 1 874493 70 7

CONTENTS

LIST OF FIGURES

1   INTRODUCTION

One of the principal objectives of good government is to achieve and maintain civil order. Order, stability and security are the foundations upon which prosperity, liberty and quality of life are built. It is, however, clear that this is not easy to achieve – a glance around the world today, or backwards at human history, shows that in many respects civil tumult and collective violence appear to be a more usual social state than public order and tranquillity.

Why do groups of people turn to collective violence? Unfortunately, as with so many questions about human behaviour, there is no simple answer. There do, however, seem to be some common factors in the places where collective violence occurs, the circumstances in which it is likely and the people who participate in them. This paper suggests that certain 'conflict variables' may be worth examining. It is possible to identify six factors which appear to underly increased levels of conflict in British cities, manifest during the last decade in civil disorder, escalating levels of crime, a growth in the hidden economy, rising use of drugs and falling levels of co-operation with the police.

The six variables are the effectiveness of government programmes, identity with the polity, opportunities for political participation, voluntary consent, views of state legitimacy and perceptions of social justice. A decrease in these factors leads to greater conflict. Furthermore, a decrease in one of these factors may produce adverse effects on other. For example, decreased effectiveness of inner-city policies leads to less identity, consent and legitimacy. Disappointment at continued relative deprivation may lead to lower participation and increased feelings of injustice.

In these circumstances, violence and conflict grows but the use of the police to suppress it often merely exacerbates matters. If the police try to manage conflict by using coercive methods, so the people who experience this feel a greater sense of injustice and less identity, and they further withdraw their consent. So the spiral continues.

These variables are affected by basic grievances and conditions in the deprived areas of British cities. Four such characteristics can be identified: high unemployment, social deprivation, political exclusion and powerlessness and mistrust of, and hostility to, the police. A fifth factor which is often present is racial disadvantage and discrimination.

The paper begins by stressing the long history of concern with order and cites examples from Britain's turbulent history. It then highlights the differing conceptions of human nature which determine the political perspectives on public disorder. Various explanations for riots are outlined before turning to look at the six variables affecting public order. The paper briefly examines the police role in managing urban problems and finally concludes that there remains a high potential in certain areas for conflict and for its escalation into serious disorder.

2   PUBLIC DISORDER IN BRITAIN

There is nothing new about public disorder and collective violence, nor the fear of it. However, there tends to be widespread 'historical amnesia' and the common view seems to be that society has become more disorderly and violent than it used to be. In the 'good old days', this argument suggests, people behaved themselves and did what they were told whereas today there is an increasingly lawless and disorderly society. Mrs. Thatcher even advocated a 'return to Victorian values' in the UK; however, a cursory examination of the Victorian period shows that it was characterised by frequent outbursts of civil disorder.

Fears About Indiscipline and Insubordination

A key word in such discussions of the past is 'discipline'. There is a widespread view, propagated in certain newspapers and by some politicians, that modern society is increasingly 'undisciplined'. In 1985, Mr Giles Shaw, Minister of State at the Home Office, told the House of Commons (*Hansard*, Vol. 84, 23 October 1985, col. 385): 'In Britain today discipline is a dirty word. It has long since ebbed from millions of homes and it has been dragged from thousands of schools. The police stand as the main bastion of discipline and responsibility in our society.'

The long tradition of concern about growing disorder and lawlessness in Britain was highlighted in Geoffrey Pearson's book *Hooligan!* (1983). This preoccupation can be traced backwards for at least 250 years. In 1981, in the *Daily Express*, Mr G. Gale stated: 'Over the past twenty years or so, there has been a revulsion from authority and discipline', and yet very similar remarks had been made two decades earlier when the 1958 Conservative Party Conference was told 'over the past twenty-five years, we in this country through misguided sentiment have cast aside the word "discipline", and now we are suffering from it.' Half a century before this, the 1904 Inter-Departmental Commission on Physical Deterioration had heard evidence that 'our young people have no idea of discipline or subordination.'

Despite Mrs. Margaret Thatcher's views of Victorian Britain, during the nineteenth century there was considerable concern about the rise in crime and disorder, particularly assault and street robbery. Much of this was put down to declining standards of behaviour and discipline of young people and H. Worsley, in his book entitled *Juvenile Depravity* (1849), declared 'Insubordination to parental authority, leading to insubordination to all authority is ... very general'. In 1843, Lord Ashley told Parliament 'the morals of children are tenfold worse than formerly', and fifteen years earlier, in a book rather melodramatically entitled *The Last Days: A Discourse on the Evil Character of These Our Times* (1828), E. Irving had reported 'Children who have been brought up within these thirty years, have nothing like the same reverence or submission to their parents ... This is the chief cause of the increase in crime'.

However, fifty years earlier indiscipline and the failure of parents to bring their children up properly had also been a cause of concern. In 1776, in his book *Solitude in Imprisonment*, J. Hanway had reported that 'We have been for some years in an undisciplined state ... it is impossible to govern people without the exertion of parental authority'. A generation earlier, Daniel Defoe (1730) had addressed a pamphlet to the Lord Mayor of London in which he expressed great anxiety:

> The Whole City, My Lord, is alarm'd and uneasy ... the Citizens are no longer secure within their own Walls, or safe even in passing their Streets, but are robbed, insulted and abused ... and such mischiefs are done within the Bounds of your Government as never were practised here before (at least not to such a degree) and which, if suffered to go on, will call for Armies, not Magistrates, to suppress it.

Britain's Turbulent Past

As the collective violence in Britain in the 1980s was often described as 'alien to our streets' it is worth underlining the point that there have been numerous instances of civil disorder and violent protest in Britain's history. Indeed, in many respects Britain's past appears to have been remarkably turbulent (Hampton, 1984; Stevenson, 1979).

Over six hundred years ago, in 1381, England was engulfed in protests about the Poll Tax. The reaction to the new tax, coupled with other injustices, resulted in the insurrection known as the Peasants' Revolt, which threatened to topple the kingdom. No government tried to introduce a poll tax again until 1989–90 when again there were serious disturbances.

In the eighteenth century, civil commotion occurred over various grievances, such as the price of flour and bread, wages and conditions, political reform, the Militia Act, enclosures and turnpikes, and excise duties. The most notable disorders were the anti-Catholic Gordon Riots in June 1780, as a result of which 285 people died and a further 25 were hanged. During the last century, violent disorders included Luddism, the post-Napoleonic Wars disturbances, rural riots such as the Captain Swing and the Rebecca disorders, and the Sunday Trading riots of 1855. The usual course when civil disorder erupted was to call in the armed forces. In 1812, Robert Southey was not even sure that the army could be relied upon (Halevy, 1912, p. 292):

> At this time nothing but the Army preserves us from the most dreadful of all calamities, an insurrection of the poor against the rich, and how long the Army may be depended upon is a question which I scarcely dare ask myself.

A significant cause of disorder in the nineteenth century was the demand for political reform. Many other violent disorders were associated with social grievances, unemployment or lack of political representation. In the disturbance in Trafalgar Square on 'Bloody Sunday', 13 November 1887, police clashed with unemployed people, leaving 3 dead and 200 injured.

In 1908 a parliamentary select committee reported that since 1869 troops had been ordered to intervene in 24 separate disturbances, and twice they had been ordered to fire. The periods before and after the First World War were also characterised by extensive disorder, over issues such as votes for women, home rule for Ireland, and industrial disputes. In 1910 troops were again called out to handle disorder, this time at Tonypandy, in the Rhondda, and the next year during violent clashes in Liverpool and Llanelli, four people were shot.

In 1919, disorders took place in areas such as Luton, Wolverhampton, Coventry and Swindon. Race riots occurred in Cardiff, where three people were shot dead, Plymouth, Newport, the East End of London and Liverpool, where Charles Wootton was killed (Jenkinson, 1993). A strike by the police in Liverpool in August 1919 resulted in widespread disorder and tanks on the streets. Despite frequent assertions to the contrary, the 1930s were years of considerable disorder with significant unrest and violence every year – with good reason the 1930s earned the title 'the devil's decade' (Benyon and Solomos, 1987, pp. 38–41).

Although British cities have a long history of disorder, the period from 1945 until 1980 was characterised by relative public tranquillity. During these thirty-five years there were, of course, many instances of violent behaviour and a number of 'moral panics', such as those over teddy-boys in the 1950s and the mods and rockers in the 1960s (Cohen, 1973; Hall and Jefferson, 1976). In August 1958, racial attacks and anti-black riots occurred in Nottingham and North Kensington.

The 1970s experienced great public concern over 'mugging' (Hall, Critcher et al., 1978; Benyon, 1986a) and also over football hooliganism (Dunning et al., 1987; Ingham, 1978). It was, furthermore, a decade when considerable anxiety was expressed over violent picketing, such as that at Saltley Coke Depot in February 1972 and at Grunwick Photographic Laboratories between August 1976 and Autumn 1977 (Clutterbuck, 1980). However, from the end of the Second World War until 1980 there were no riots in British cities – as distinct from those in Northern Ireland – to compare with the unrest which occurred subsequently.

Recent Riots in Britain

The inner-city riots of 1980 and 1981 were the turning point. By 1984, the Metropolitan Police Commissioner was reporting that there were 'many mini-riots which had the potential to escalate to Brixton 1981 proportions' and he added: 'London is nowadays a very volatile city' (*Guardian*, 17 October 1984; Benyon, 1984, pp. 53, 61 and 241). Further serious rioting occurred in 1985 and this was repeated in subsequent years, notably in 1991. There was also major disorder associated with industrial disputes, for example in the miners' strike of 1984–85 and the Wapping print dispute. In addition, as previously mentioned, there were violent protests about the poll tax, most notably the events in Trafalgar Square on 31 March 1990.

It is worth being reminded briefly of the terrible extent of the disorder during the last decade or so (Keith, 1993). In Brixton, on Saturday 11 April 1981, during nearly six hours of violence, arson and looting, 279 police officers and at least 45 members of the public were injured, 61 private and 56 police vehicles were damaged or destroyed and 145 premises were damaged, 28 of them by fire (Scarman, 1981). On Friday 3 July 1981, in the Liverpool 8 district of Merseyside, an apparently minor incident sparked off rioting which lasted until Monday 6 July. On the Sunday night alone 282 police officers were injured and some never recovered sufficiently to return to duty. For the first time ever in Britain, CS gas was fired at the rioters by the police. Looting and arson were widespread, and the damage was estimated at some £10 million.

On Monday 9 September 1985, in the Lozells Road area of Handsworth, Birmingham, major disorder resulted in the deaths of two people, reported injuries to 122 other people, mainly police, and damaged property the value of which was put at £7.5 million. During the weekend 28–29 September 1985, in Brixton, 724 major crimes were reported, 43 members of the public and ten police officers were injured, and 230 arrests were made. The most serious of the 1985 disorders occurred at Broadwater Farm Estate, in Tottenham, London. During a night of extraordinary violence Police Constable Keith Blakelock was stabbed to death, 20 members of the public and 223 police officers were injured and 47 cars and some buildings were burned. Guns were fired at the police, causing injuries to several officers and reporters.

The Trafalgar Square disorder of 31 March 1990 also resulted in many injuries and extensive damage to property (Waddington, 1992). Rioting occurred in 1991 in places as diverse as Blackbird Leys, Oxford (29 August– 4 September), Ely Estate, Cardiff (30 August–1 September), Handsworth, Birmingham (2 September) and the Meadow Well Estate, Newcastle (9–12 September) (Campbell, 1993). Large numbers of injuries, crimes and damage to property were reported. Further disorder was reported in various cities and suburban estates in 1992 and 1993.

3   POLITICAL ARGUMENT ABOUT LAW AND ORDER

It is easy to ask the simple question 'why do people riot?' but rather less easy to provide a straightforward answer. However, in the aftermath of each instance of disorder in Britain since 1980 there have been many pundits, politicians and police officers prepared to provide easy answers and simple solutions.

Conceptions of Human Nature

At the root of much of the contemporary debate about law and order are different conceptions of human nature. At one end of the spectrum are the 'pessimists', or 'realists', who believe that people are by nature self-seeking and greedy. On the other side are the 'optimists', or 'idealists', who believe that humans are not by nature bad but largely behave according to the circumstances and environment in which they live – so social, political, economic and cultural factors are fundamental.

The liberal and radical perspectives focus on the basic flaws in social and political arrangements, whereas the conservative interpretation stresses the basic flaws in human nature. This point was made by the Home Secretary in the debate in the House of Commons on 23 October 1985. He drew attention to:

> The excitement of forming and belonging to a mob, the evident excitement of violence leading to the fearsome crimes that we have seen reported and the greed that leads to looting ... to explain all those things in terms of deprivation and suffering is to ignore some basic and ugly facts about human nature.

This realistic or pessimistic view was set out by Niccolo Machiavelli (1469–1527) and Thomas Hobbes (1588–1679). In *The Prince* Machiavelli argued that the sovereign is justified in resorting to treachery and violence in order to maintain order and authority over the wicked population. Hobbes saw humans as being essentially egotistical, motivated by the pursuit of pleasure and the avoidance of pain, and above all by their own self-preservation. He used the metaphor of the state of nature to illustrate the condition in which people would exist without strong government. It would be a state of constant war between selfish individuals and the life of each person would be 'poor, nasty, brutish and short'. In his greatest work, *Leviathan,* Hobbes outlined this conception and argued that it was in the interests of all people to live under a strong sovereign and the rule of law.

The idealist view is represented by the writings of Jean-Jacques Rousseau (1712–1778) and Karl Marx (1818–1883). Rousseau's philosophy was set out in the *Social Contract* and *Emile*, both published in 1762. He believed that humans are good by nature but have been corrupted by society. In sharp contrast to Hobbes' view, Rousseau argued that in the state of nature each individual was happy, good and free but now 'everywhere he is in chains'. It is thus not human nature that is to blame for vice, crime and disorder but rather society itself.

Perceptions of Crime and Disorder

The realist view of human nature forms the basis of the conservative perspective on law and order, while the idealist conception underlies the liberal and radical perspectives. The different political arguments and prescriptions about law and order derive from these contrasting views of human beings, and all too often discussions about the causes of collective violence are 'dialogues of the deaf' based on these fundamentally different views of the nature of human beings.

The **conservative perspective** tends to adopt an authoritarian, tough-minded approach, which emphasises discipline, deterrence and punishment. Support for the rule of law, and for the law enforcers, is stressed and permissiveness is rejected. Given that people are inherently self-seeking, the fear of punishment is necessary to deter them from behaving illegally. The theory of deterrence is central to this approach: people are rational and will calculate that the costs of being caught and punished outweigh the benefits of the crime. However, for this theory to work the punishment must be sufficiently great and their chances of being caught and convicted must also be high.

It is also important for parents, schools and communities to bring young people up to behave properly and to respect the law and those in authority – much of people's behaviour is based on habit and good habits must be established for the young. According to the conservative perspective, without the firm guidelines provided by family values, religion and the rule of law, young people in particular may be seduced by vice and pleasure-seeking. The permissiveness of the 1960s, and the subsequent tolerance of previously deviant behaviour, has led to increased crime and lawlessness.

CONSERVATIVE PERSPECTIVE	LIBERAL/RADICAL PERSPECTIVE
authoritarian	liberal
tough-minded	tender-minded
punishment	rehabilitation
deterrence through penalties	remove social causes
emphasis on police powers	emphasis on civil liberties
stresses discipline	stresses education
rejects 'permissiveness'	rejects authoritarianism
stresses 'rule of law'	stresses 'social justice'

Figure 1: Different Approaches to Law and Order

The **liberal approach** tends to see economic, social and cultural deprivation as the major causes of crime and disorder, with people behaving in this way either because they are deprived of material goods and status or because they learn it as they grow up. These explanations tend to assert that behaviour is largely conditioned by environmental factors such as family background, material conditions, housing, educational opportunities, cultural experiences and the influence of the mass media.

The liberal perspective tends to adopt a more tender-minded approach, which emphasises the need to create the conditions in which people will behave properly. Instead of discipline it stresses responsibility; instead of deterrence it emphasises the need to win consent; instead of punishment it stresses rewards and rehabilitation. According to this view, the law is not a neutral set of rules but favours those who have possessions and power. Law and order is a question of justice, rather than the 'rule of law', and this must include social justice, in the form of removing excessive inequalities and assisting less favoured members of society. The theory of deterrence is accepted to some extent but the theory only works when people have something to lose and some view of the future. Too many people, according to the liberal perspective, have such a small material and social stake that punishment ceases to offer much of a deterrent. It is difficult to deprive people who are already deprived.

Alongside decent living conditions, the role of education is also important, but this must be education for citizenship in a just society. The liberal approach sees ignorance as a principal cause of crime, disorder and violence. It is through knowledge and understanding that people can enter into society as full citizens. It is absurd to blame 'permissiveness' for increased crime and lawlessness, according to this view. The need is not to curtail people's individual freedom, but rather to educate them to act responsibly and create the conditions in which decent behaviour can develop. The liberal approach emphasises the importance of civil liberties and warns against increased police powers and more draconian punishment. According to this perspective, crime must be tackled by society as a whole, and giving the police more powers is likely to lead to a decrease in many people's willingness to co-operate with them, while rehabilitation of criminals is more likely to produce results rather than tougher punishment.

In many respects the **radical perspective** can be seen as broadly similar to the liberal approach. Crime and disorder are generally viewed as the inevitable results of unfair economic and social arrangements. Power and opportunity are not equally available to everyone – indeed, certain groups are systematically excluded from full participation in the fruits of society. The consent of such people will not readily be forthcoming, and crime and disorder are likely to be the result of this exclusion and deprivation. Like the liberal approach, the radical perspective holds out a degree of optimism for the generation of a 'good society' through the exercise of social policy and political action, although the prescriptions generally involve a much stronger shift towards equality and the removal of privilege.

4   THE POLITICS OF DISORDER

In order to examine the various explanations which are put forward to account for riots, the liberal and radical perspectives can be grouped together. Both focus on 'basic flaws' in society and its political arrangements, highlighting social injustice, inadequate institutions and the maldistribution of resources and political power as causes of disorder.

Liberal and Radical Explanations

Riots are seen as a result of the failure of structures to accommodate demands and to satisfy the grievances and expectations of certain groups, and as the result of unfair treatment. Some theorists have drawn attention to *poverty and hardship* as causes of collective violence, but a number of historical studies have shown that participants in disorder are often not the most deprived people (Rude, 1981).

A more plausible theory emphasises *relative deprivation*, where people feel that they do not have that which they need or deserve. This notion is associated with the idea of *unrealised expectations* as a cause of discontent, a crisis occurring when rising expectations are thwarted by a downturn in their satisfaction (Davies, 1979). People unable to achieve goals which they believe should be attainable experience a build-up in tension which eventually explodes in an uncontrollable outburst of anger (Dollard, 1974; Gurr, 1970). This is cathartic, so that after the violence the tension is dissipated, although it may begin to build up again.

These theories pinpoint deprivation as the fundamental cause of rioting, but the violence itself is seen as a furious outburst. Others have argued that while deprivation is an underlying problem, the violent protest should be seen as rational and purposeful action by those who have been systematically excluded from full participation in society. Thus, the explanation for disorder is *political exclusion*, as well as disadvantage. Riots are the means of forcing demands, which otherwise would be ignored, onto the political agenda (Bachrach and Baratz, 1970). Similarly, it has been argued that *lack of political voice* is a key factor. Political voice is important for the healthy functioning of the political system, but many of the most active, able and articulate residents have migrated from the inner-city areas – just the people who would have complained, organised and agitated for improvements and extra resources. The result is a voiceless and frustrated population (Hirschman, 1970).

The term *political marginalisation* has been used to describe the position of those who are powerless and deprived, and the notion of *alienation* has also been applied by some theorists to characterise the demoralisation and estrangement from society and its values of those who suffer social rejection and disadvantage (Lea and Young, 1984). Others have suggested that *weak social integration* is a cause of disorder. This results, it is claimed, from poverty, poor housing and unemployment, and concomitant high levels of crime, which lead to a demoralised population in the area. Accompanied by a high turnover of local residents, these factors cause a decline in consensus on values and weakened social ties. Thus disadvantage leads to a social disintegration with a high potential for outbreaks of violent disturbances.

Another explanation highlights *perceptions of injustice* as the central factor. If people believe that the outcomes of decisions or the behaviour of those in authority are unjust, they may become increasingly resentful and angry. The anger increases until one further, often seemingly small, incident of unjust behaviour results in a violent reaction. Racial discrimination and unemployment are likely to cause feelings of injustice, as is improper police conduct.

In the aftermath of the collective violence in Britain in 1985, some police officers favoured explanations drawn from the social and political flaws category. Colin Couch, for example, who was Chief Superintendent in Tottenham, said that social disadvantage and unemployment were important factors. Jonathan Sayeed, Conservative MP for Bristol East, said: 'Those who feel rejected by society will tend to reject the rules of that society'. John Fraser, Labour MP for Norwood, the constituency in which much of Brixton falls, stated: 'It is impossible to divorce the catastrophic cuts in housing, the catastrophic increase in unemployment and the catastrophic cuts in all sorts of services, in the constituency and borough that I represent, from what has happened in that area, where deep hatred, disillusion, despair and alienation lie beneath the surface and are the cause of these riots.'

Conservative Explanations

In the United States these were termed the 'riff-raff' theories of riots, since they see riots as being perpetrated by the most worthless and disreputable people – the riff-raff of society. Riff-raff explanations tend to focus on individuals' wilful behaviour, or on their weakness and gullibility. Rioters are seen as people indulging in *criminal activity*, motivated by a desire to loot and rob, and rationally choosing to do this having calculated the costs and benefits (Tullock, 1971). The Home Secretary said after the Handsworth disorder that it was 'not a social phenomenon but crimes': it was 'not a cry for help but a cry for loot'. Another explanation is that *excitement* is a reason for disorders: young people in particular are said to derive 'fun value' from them (Banfield, 1968). Rioting is thus seen as similar to football hooliganism.

Another view suggests that *crowd behaviour* explains disorder. If a group of people gather together, their behaviour may degenerate into mob or 'mindless' violence (Le Bon, 1960). This is most likely to happen, suggests another theory, if there is *social disorganisation* as a result of community disruption, perhaps brought about by redevelopment or an influx of newcomers to an area. This introduces the impact of immigration, and the effects of 'alien' cultures.

An associated explanation pinpoints *moral degeneration* or a *decline in respect for the rule of law* as causes of riots and crime in general (Clutterbuck, 1980 and 1983). This holds that values and modes of behaviour have deteriorated and traditional social controls are no longer effective in preventing violence. Norman Tebbit, Conservative Party Chairman, said after the 1985 Tottenham riots in London that they were the result of 'wickedness', and he later suggested that the moral degeneration was a legacy of the permissive society of the 1960s. This decline is often blamed on families and schools.

The media may be held responsible for the perceived erosion of values and traditional restraints on anti-social behaviour, and television in particular is seen by some as *legitimising violence* as a form of protest. This links with a further explanation of rioting as *contagious behaviour*, which may be transmitted from one area to others in the form of 'copycat' disorders (Spilerman, 1976). In 1985, for example, it was suggested that the riots in Britain were a result of the television broadcasts of black protests in South Africa.

A final, and very common, theory of rioting is that it is engineered by extremists and subversives. The *conspiracy theory*, that agitators are fostering discontent, appears to have been advanced to explain almost all the disorders that have occurred in Britain since the Gordon Riots of 1780 (Murdock 1984). In 1985, some senior police officers said that the urban riots in Britain were planned, either by political extremists (or 'militant insurrectionaries' as Sir Eldon Griffiths, MP, put it) or by drug dealers. The media seized on both these propositions. To take one (ludicrous) example, in its 'Tottenham Riot Special' edition, the *Daily Express* led with a story of how 'a hand-picked death squad', consisting of 'street-fighting experts trained in Moscow and Libya', had 'acted on the orders of crazed left-wing extremists'!

The main shortcoming of the conspiracy theory is that there is rarely, if ever, any plausible evidence to support it. Both the Kerner Commission and Lord Scarman specifically dismissed the suggestion that the disorders were the result of a plan or conspiracy. Lord Scarman was emphatic: 'They originated spontaneously. There was no premeditation or plan.'

Common Characteristics of Riot Areas

Lord Scarman's inquiry into the 1981 disorders in the Brixton area of London, like the 1967 Kerner Commission's inquiry into the United States disorders, tended to adopt a liberal perspective. Scarman reported that the disorder occurred in the context of political, social and economic disadvantage, including high levels of unemployment, poor housing and widespread racial discrimination. Black people, he found, suffered from the same deprivations as whites 'but much more acutely'. The despair of many young blacks led them to feel rejected by British society.

A crucial factor was the hostility between young people in Brixton and the police, who were seen as pursuing, abusing and harassing them and as representing a regime which was 'insensitive to their plight'. Lord Scarman reported: 'Where deprivation and frustration exist on the scale to be found among the young black people of Brixton, the probability of disorder must, therefore, be strong.'

It does seem that in the 1980s and 1990s, as so often in the past, the areas in which disorder occurred in the UK shared certain common characteristics. There seem to be four characteristics which are common to all the areas where collective violence has occurred in British cities:

(1)   Unemployment was high, and particularly affected young people. For example, in autumn 1985 the unemployment rate in Britain was 13% but in Birmingham it was 20.8%; in Handsworth it was 34.8%. Of those who left school in 1984, 18% of whites and 15.8% of Asians, but only 4.9% of Afro-Caribbeans, had found a job a year later. Youth unemployment in general in Handsworth was 50%, while on Broadwater Farm Estate it was 60%.

(2)   Deprivation was widespread: environmental decay, poor educational and social service provision, inadequate recreational facilities and high levels of crime were problems. In particular, housing was often substandard and a source of great distress. For example, the 1981 census showed that whereas under 1% of households in Britain was overcrowded, in Birmingham the figure was 6% and in Handsworth it was over 15%.

(3)   Political exclusion and powerlessness were widespread, in that there were few institutions, opportunities and resources for articulating grievances and bringing pressure to bear on those with political power. Decisions were imposed upon these communities through a 'top-down' approach by the professionals in local or central government, or by agencies such as the urban development corporations. This lack of political voice led to a growing sense of frustration and disaffection.

(4)   Mistrust of, and hostility to, the police was evident among certain sections of the public, particularly the young. There was disquiet about police tactics, such as stop and search, and allegations were frequently made about harassment, abuse and assault (Smith, 1983; Reiner, 1985; Benyon, 1986). Lord Scarman found a 'loss of confidence by significant sections' of the Lambeth public. The incidents of misconduct which he found, led to a spiral of decline in relations so that many young people had become 'indignant and resentful against the police, suspicious of everything they did' (Scarman, 1981, para 4.1).

In addition, a fifth factor was evident in many of the areas in which disorder occurred:

(5)   Racial disadvantage and discrimination were major afflictions. A significant proportion of the population in many of the areas in which rioting occurred was African–Caribbean or Asian. These were the people who experienced social and economic disadvantage particularly acutely, and who also suffered from racial discrimination, racist abuse and sometimes physical attacks (Brown, 1984; Benyon, 1984, pp. 163–229). Lord Scarman (1981, para 9.1) reported:

> Racial disadvantage is a fact of current British life. It was, I am equally sure, a significant factor in the causation of the Brixton disorders. Urgent action is needed if it is not to become an endemic ineradicable disease threatening the very survival of our society.

Variables Affecting Public Order

The five common characteristics indicate the grievances and context which may give rise to urban unrest, but how are they translated into disorder and violent action? Clearly, in Britain and in other countries, people may experience these forms of disadvantage without taking part in riots and protest. They are conditions under which unrest may occur, but it is necessary to examine the ways in which they erode social controls and restraints on violent disorder.

There seem to be six variables which may help to explain how unemployment, deprivation, political exclusion, police hostility and racism develop into urban conflict. These variables are governmental effectiveness, citizen identity, participation and consent, and people's perceptions of the regime's legitimacy and justness. Under certain circumstances, violence and disorder become increasingly likely.

It can be hypothesised that the probability of urban conflict rises as the effectiveness of government policies declines, as levels of identity with the polity decrease, as opportunities for political participation fall, as levels of voluntary consent decline, as perceptions of the regime's legitimacy decrease and as experiences of injustice rise.

(i)   Ineffective Government Programmes

The attempts to tackle inner-city problems, in Britain as in many other countries, have been largely ineffective. The agencies and institutions involved have not functioned effectively and resources have not been allocated efficiently, the deterioration in urban conditions has continued, and consequently promises, and people's expectations, have not been met.

Discontent is likely to be strong when there is a gap between what people experience and that which they have been led to expect. Offe (1984, p. 144) has pointed to 'the increasingly visible conflict between the promise and the experience, form and content, of state policies' and this can lead to 'a revolution of rising frustrations' (Millikan and Blackmer, 1961, p. 41).

The failure of government policies may affect people's identity with the polity, their view of the legitimacy of its rules and agents and their voluntary consent to its actions. As a Home Office study (Field, 1982, p. 33) pointed out:

> Where any social group perceives government institutions as being indifferent to its needs, the authority and legitimacy of social controls ultimately promulgated by those same institutions will be increasingly questioned.

(ii)   Questions of Identity

An important aspect of any society is the extent to which its members identify with the polity, the political system and prevailing values (Binder et al., 1971; Grew, et al., 1978). Central questions are whether people share an identity in terms of common norms and values, and whether their group identity is more salient than their identification with the polity.

If the attempts by governments to tackle unemployment, racial discrimination, and inner-city disadvantage are regarded as ineffective and lacking in commitment, the level of identification which people so affected have with the political system and its predominant values may diminish. Why should people who are excluded identify with the system which is excluding them? Lowenthal (1984, p. 34) has argued that there is an 'underlying cultural crisis' which is visible in 'the increasingly defective functioning of the process of socialisation and of the formation of identity'.

Identity with *group* norms may become pre-eminent if the integrity of society's rules, institutions and values becomes undermined. Some behaviour regarded as deviant elsewhere in society may become accepted within particular groups, leading for example to increased levels of crime or a willingness to participate in violent action. Evidence gathered in the aftermath of the US riots in the 1960s revealed considerable support for the rioters, particularly amongst other black Americans in large cities (McCord and Howard, 1968, pp. 24–27; Sears and McConahay, 1973).

Similar findings were reported after the riots in England in 1981. A poll of young people showed that 28% considered the disorders were justified, and 44% agreed with the statement 'violence to bring about political change can be justified' [41% disagreed; 15% did not know] (Benyon and Solomos, 1987, p.185). These findings were in marked contrast with polls of the whole population which showed strong disapproval of the riots.

A decrease in people's identity with the values and institutions of the political system is likely to result in diminished consent and perhaps a repudiation of political authority. It may affect the effectiveness of government policies and it has implications for political participation.

(iii)   Opportunities for Participation

The importance of citizen participation in political systems is widely recognised. Political participation is a principal method whereby demands are articulated, and it is a vital means of legitimising the government and the regime, and of ensuring voluntary obedience. However, participation is not limited to formal channels, and indeed need not itself be legitimate. Many of the disturbances and riots in Britain's past are now regarded by historians as 'collective bargaining by riot' (Hobsbawm, 1959), whereby workers could bring pressure to bear on their employers, or more generally as a means of political participation for those with no other opportunities of political voice.

Deprived urban areas tend to have few institutions, such as pressure groups and political parties, through which participation can be channelled and demands made. However, unless the development of opportunities and institutions for participation keeps pace with the underlying pressure for the articulation of demands problems for the political order may ensue. Participation is important not only to legitimise the regime, and to aid the effectiveness of its performance, but also to enhance identification with the polity. Institutional participation facilitates integration and also lowers the probability of dramatic non-institutional participation, or voice, in the form of violent protest. Huntingdon's point (1968, p.198) is well made:

> In any institutionalised society the participation of new groups reduces tensions; through participation, new groups are assimilated into the political order.

The implications of a lack of political institutions and procedures in inner-city areas may be serious; the results may be alienation, withdrawal, resentment or anger.

(iv)   Consent on the Ebb

Opportunities for participation are related to the level of consent. Citizens are more likely to agree to comply with decisions about which they have formally voiced their opinions. Consent is also influenced by other considerations such as the legitimacy of the system, and identity with the polity, and institutional participation is likely to be important in establishing these factors. According to Almond and Verba (1963, p. 253), their five-nation study revealed that:

> The opportunity to participate in political decisions is associated with greater satisfaction with that system and with greater general loyalty ... the sense of ability to participate in politics appears to increase the legitimacy of a system.

Participation is a feature of the process of socialisation, whereby identification with the prevailing values, rules and procedures is developed. It is a means of generating loyalty and allegiance to the political system, and so is important in determining consent and acquiescence. The low level of participation in institutionalised processes in Britain's deprived areas may thus detrimentally affect the extent to which citizens voluntarily consent to government policies, to the state's agents, and to the rules and procedures of the regime.

There is considerable evidence for the decrease in levels of voluntary consent in urban areas. This may become manifest in falling levels of co-operation with the police, eruptions of violent disorder or as a refusal to comply with directives and rules. This will adversely affect the way government can be carried out. If consent declines, the government and its agencies may find it necessary to employ coercion. But coercion is expensive and may also be ineffective or even counterproductive. The use of coercion may suppress disorder temporarily, but research suggests that these sorts of measures often result in even greater frustration and feelings of injustice leading to further outbreaks of violent disorders (Buss, 1961; Gurr, 1968; Johnson, 1968; National Advisory Committee, 1976). Furthermore, coercion may undermine the legitimacy of the regime.

(v)   Perceptions of Legitimacy

Essentially, legitimacy is the quality of being lawful or right. A claim that something is legitimate rests upon the assertion that it is proper according to rules or principles, and a government and its behaviour can be evaluated in this way. Dahrendorf (1980, p. 397) offered the following view:

> A government is legitimate if what it does is right both in the sense of complying with certain fundamental principles, and in that of being in line with prevailing cultural values.

The behaviour and actions of a government are important sources of its legitimacy. Effective performance is a means whereby citizens will ascribe legitimacy to the government and to the system, and so too is identity with the polity and its values. Institutional participation is a means of realising identity, effectiveness and consent, but it is also directly a source of legitimacy, through elections, groups and other organisations. The legitimacy of the British political order is likely to be severely strained as a result of racial discrimination and disadvantage, urban decay and dereliction, unemployment, political exclusion and alleged police misconduct. The declining levels of identity, and the increasingly wide gulf between people's experiences and prospects in deprived areas and those elsewhere, undermine consensus, confidence and legitimacy.

It is worth noting that the historian Keith Thomas (1978, p. 64) has reported that in England crises of legitimacy have only arisen:

> When the regime fails to deliver other goods expected of it – law and order, religious toleration, political participation or social justice.

(vi)   Social Injustice: the Central Thread

A number of commentators have suggested that perceptions of justice are important in determining whether civil disorder occurs. If people believe that the behaviour of those in authority, or of others in a position of power over them, is not just they may be prepared to take matters into their own hands. For example, many violent riots in British history seem to have been protecting established rights, standards of living or working practices. Thompson (1968) has shown that the leaders of the disorders were often regarded as heroes and the direct action was seen as just. The notion of justice is important in explaining the behaviour not only of those who rioted, but also of those who either tacitly or openly supported them. According to Thompson (1971, p. 76):

> The men and women in the crowd were informed by the belief that they were defending traditional rights and customs; and in general, that they were supported by the wider consensus of the community.

Perceptions of justice involve the idea of fairness. Feelings of relative deprivation may give rise to a perception of injustice, as may experiences of behaviour by those in authority which is biased or partial. If people experience police behaviour which they perceive to be prejudiced or abusive they will feel that they have been unjustly treated. Injustice is a key factor in mobilising protest. Its significance was stressed by Thomas Carlyle in 1839 (Carlyle, 1892, p. 23):

> It is not what a man outwardly has or wants that constitutes the happiness or misery of him. Nakedness, hunger, distress of all kinds, death itself have been cheerfully suffered when the heart was right. It is the feeling of injustice that is insupportable to all men ... No man can bear it or ought to bear it.

Racial discrimination, prolonged unemployment, poor housing and other forms of urban deprivation are likely to cause feelings of injustice. Urban unrest is a violent *reaction* to events and experiences. The tinder is created by the underlying conditions, but it is ignited by a particular event which provides the spark. Almost inevitably the immediate precipitant event which triggers unrest involves police officers.

In the recent British riots most, if not all, the major outbreaks of disorder were triggered by an incident involving the police and black people (Waddington et al., 1989). In each case, the police action seems to have been perceived as another example of unjust treatment, which then led to a violent reaction. Figure 2 indicates the apparent causes and 'flashpoints' or triggers of major British riots between 1980 and 1991 (see Brightmore, 1992).

Social injustice is the central thread running through urban conflict. Above all, it is experiences or perceptions of injustice which may develop into a violent urban disorder.

5   THE ROLE OF THE POLICE

The United Kingdom has traditionally been widely regarded as 'an outstanding example of successful integration – almost, as it were, the first "melting pot"' (Urwin, 1982, pp. 19–20). The UK was viewed as homogeneous, with widespread consent, a high level of governmental legitimacy and effectiveness, and common values.

However, since 1980 increased division, social disintegration and conflict have become increasingly within English cities. These trends are also evident is many other cities in Europe and elsewhere. The inner city, it is said, is 'a place apart'. The difficulties of managing conflict in such areas

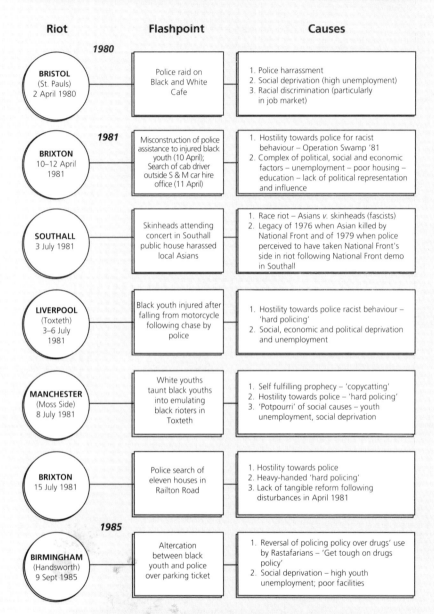

Riot	Flashpoint	Causes
1980		
BRISTOL (St. Pauls) 2 April 1980	Police raid on Black and White Cafe	1. Police harrassment 2. Social deprivation (high unemployment) 3. Racial discrimination (particularly in job market)
1981 **BRIXTON** 10–12 April 1981	Misconstruction of police assistance to injured black youth (10 April); Search of cab driver outside S & M car hire office (11 April)	1. Hostility towards police for racist behaviour – Operation Swamp '81 2. Complex of political, social and economic factors – unemployment – poor housing – education – lack of political representation and influence
SOUTHALL 3 July 1981	Skinheads attending concert in Southall public house harassed local Asians	1. Race riot – Asians *v.* skinheads (fascists) 2. Legacy of 1976 when Asian killed by National Front and of 1979 when police perceived to have taken National Front's side in riot following National Front demo in Southall
LIVERPOOL (Toxteth) 3–6 July 1981	Black youth injured after falling from motorcycle following chase by police	1. Hostility towards police racist behaviour – 'hard policing' 2. Social, economic and political deprivation and unemployment
MANCHESTER (Moss Side) 8 July 1981	White youths taunt black youths into emulating black rioters in Toxteth	1. Self fulfilling prophecy – 'copycatting' 2. Hostility towards police – 'hard policing' 3. 'Potpourri' of social causes – youth unemployment, social deprivation
BRIXTON 15 July 1981	Police search of eleven houses in Railton Road	1. Hostility towards police 2. Heavy-handed 'hard policing' 3. Lack of tangible reform following disturbances in April 1981
1985 **BIRMINGHAM** (Handsworth) 9 Sept 1985	Altercation between black youth and police over parking ticket	1. Reversal of policing policy over drugs' use by Rastafarians – 'Get tough on drugs policy' 2. Social deprivation – high youth unemployment; poor facilities

Source: Adapted from C. Brightmore, *Urban Rioting in Latter Day Britain,*
MA dissertation, CSPO, University of Leicester, 1992 (unpublished)

Figure 2: Causes and Flashpoints of British Riots, 1980–1991

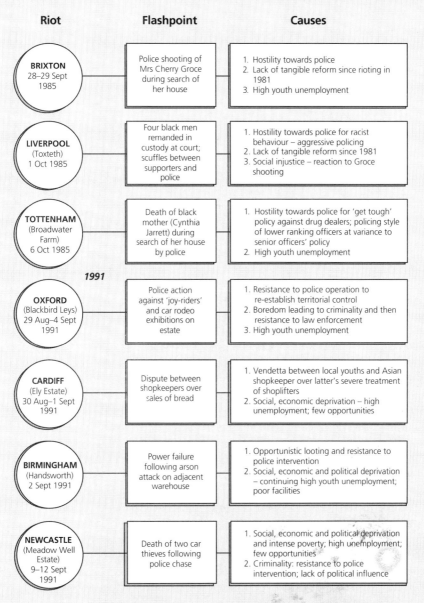

Riot	Flashpoint	Causes
BRIXTON 28–29 Sept 1985	Police shooting of Mrs Cherry Groce during search of her house	1. Hostility towards police 2. Lack of tangible reform since rioting in 1981 3. High youth unemployment
LIVERPOOL (Toxteth) 1 Oct 1985	Four black men remanded in custody at court; scuffles between supporters and police	1. Hostility towards police for racist behaviour – aggressive policing 2. Lack of tangible reform since 1981 3. Social injustice – reaction to Groce shooting
TOTTENHAM (Broadwater Farm) 6 Oct 1985	Death of black mother (Cynthia Jarrett) during search of her house by police	1. Hostility towards police for 'get tough' policy against drug dealers; policing style of lower ranking officers at variance to senior officers' policy 2. High youth unemployment
1991 **OXFORD** (Blackbird Leys) 29 Aug–4 Sept 1991	Police action against 'joy-riders' and car rodeo exhibitions on estate	1. Resistance to police operation to re-establish territorial control 2. Boredom leading to criminality and then resistance to law enforcement 3. High youth unemployment
CARDIFF (Ely Estate) 30 Aug–1 Sept 1991	Dispute between shopkeepers over sales of bread	1. Vendetta between local youths and Asian shopkeeper over latter's severe treatment of shoplifters 2. Social, economic deprivation – high unemployment; few opportunities
BIRMINGHAM (Handsworth) 2 Sept 1991	Power failure following arson attack on adjacent warehouse	1. Opportunistic looting and resistance to police intervention 2. Social, economic and political deprivation – continuing high youth unemployment; poor facilities
NEWCASTLE (Meadow Well Estate) 9–12 Sept 1991	Death of two car thieves following police chase	1. Social, economic and political deprivation and intense poverty; high unemployment; few opportunities 2. Criminality: resistance to police intervention; lack of political influence

Source: Adapted from C. Brightmore, *Urban Rioting in Latter Day Britain*, MA dissertation, CSPO, University of Leicester, 1992 (unpublished)

Figure 2: Causes and Flashpoints of British Riots, 1980–1991

were stressed by Sir Kenneth Newman (1987, p. 8), the Commissioner of the Metropolitan Police, in a speech in February 1987:

> The inner cities are the areas with the most recalcitrant social problems. They have the highest crime rates, the most widespread and most established drug abuse, and the greatest potential for serious public disorder. They are the most deprived areas, the areas with the most left-wing councils, and the places where the police have the least institutional support. They are what the tabloid press is irresistibly drawn to call the 'no-go' areas ... They present fundamental difficulties for policing. Indeed they are a challenge to the style of British policing upon which we have relied since the foundation of the Metropolitan Police in 1829.

The Commissioner's remarks suggest that the wheel is turning full circle, for the Metropolitan Police was established in order to combat conflict and disorder, rather than crime, by the 'dangerous classes' in their London 'rookeries' (Philips, 1983; Reiner, 1985). Now, as then, it appears that conflict in the inner cities must be managed by the police. But is this an effective and efficient means of maintaining the Queen's Peace? May over-reliance on the police in fact lead to greater conflict?

In the early 1980s the reliance on the police to manage conflict led to undesirable developments in the style, methods and equipment of inner-city policing (Reiner, 1985). It was claimed by some that these developments reinforced the difficulties which were experienced in policing deprived areas. Lea and Young (1984), for example, produced a model to illustrate the self-reinforcement of what they termed 'military policing'. According to the model, rising crime (particularly street crime) occurs as a result of unemployment and deprivation and the police respond by adopting proactive tactics (termed 'hard policing' by Lord Scarman and others). However, this style of policing angers and alienates bystanders and older members of the community who withdraw their co-operation from the police. The fall in information for the police makes the task of clearing up crime more difficult which then tends to lead to even more proactive 'hard' policing, which results in even greater local antipathy and less information ... and so the cycle continues.

The idea of a vicious circle of deprivation and disorder has been developed by Chris Brightmore (1992). As shown in Figure 3, his model begins with

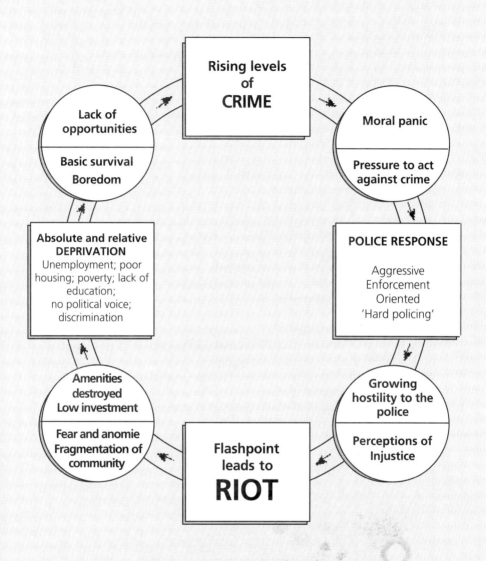

Source: Adapted from C. Brightmore, *Urban Rioting in Latter Day Britain*,
MA dissertation, CSPO, University of Leicester, 1992 (unpublished)

Figure 3: The Vicious Circle of Deprivation and Civil Disorder

the high levels of crime and he charts the developing media and public pressure on the police to take action which often results in 'aggressive enforcement-orientated' tactics and operations. Some of what occurs is perceived as unjust and sooner or later the growing hostility to the police may erupt as a riot. The result of this disorder is the destruction of local amenities, with business scared away and lower investment, leading to increased unemployment and deprivation and boredom. In such a context, increased crime occurs leading to a further police response.

What can the police do in such areas? They are not, after all, in a position to implement policies to remove the unemployment, deprivation and racial disadvantage. They can, however, take action to avoid entering the vicious downward spiral, can seek to gain increased co-operation from law-abiding members of the communities and can try to avoid triggering serious disorder (Waddington et al., 1989). Such a strategy involves patience and fortitude and can easily be set back by one unfortunate incident. Three related strands can be identified: communication, information and intelligence, and consistency.

(1)   Communication: this is two-way activity. The local community must be kept informed of police policies and approaches, and the police must listen to the views of local people. It is time-consuming but surely vital if local policing is to function as effectively as possible. Communication is a form of participation – it helps to raise identity, legitimacy and consent – and the necessary investment in it should pay dividends in terms of greater public tranquillity.

(2)   Information and Intelligence: effective communication should increase the amount of information available to the police. This needs to be processed as intelligence to aid local policing, and is important not just for preventing and detecting crime, but also for maintaining public order. As Figure 4 shows, the Metropolitan Police has developed an integrated intelligence system for community tension assessment. Despite its grand title, this appears to be a rather rudimentary system for appraising potential disorder. It is a beginning, but quite a lot more work seems necessary before it develops into an effective system. There is also the danger that the police will be seen as 'spying' on local communities and so the police should be open about the existence of such a system, explaining how it functions and why it is necessary. They should also be prepared to respond to community criticisms and suggestions.

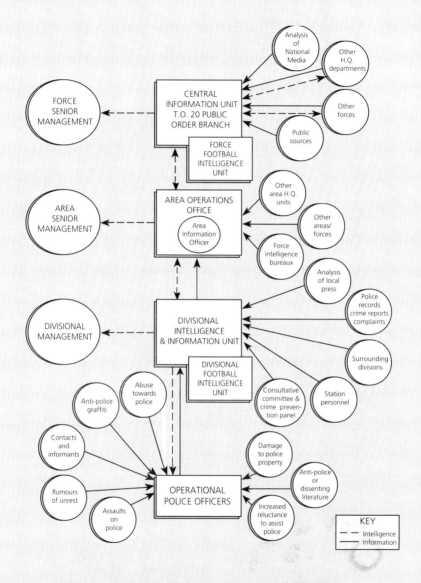

Source: Adapted from C. Brightmore, *Urban Rioting in Latter Day Britain*,
MA dissertation, CSPO, University of Leicester, 1992 (unpublished)

**Figure 4: The Metropolitan Police Integrated Intelligence System
for Community Tension Assessment**

(3)   **Consistency:** at the local level, public order is largely maintained through the application of unwritten rules and conventions. Of course, the law itself is important, but so too are the local 'rules' of acceptable behaviour. These vary widely between different areas, so that what may be acceptable on the streets of one area may not be acceptable on the streets of another. Various studies have suggested that if an inconsistent approach is adopted – so that behaviour which was tolerated yesterday is not acceptable today – public disorder problems are more likely.

The police need to be aware of the conflict variables identified earlier and should try to improve matters. This means taking action to increase levels of effectiveness, identity, participation, and perceptions of legitimacy and fairness and justice. If they manage to raise these factors the police will secure higher levels of trust and consent, and the likelihood of disorder will diminish. Perhaps, above all, increased community participation in police policy making and discussions provides the key.

6   THE CONTINUING POTENTIAL FOR DISORDER

History shows that the usual response to violent protest and riots has been repression and coercion. History also reveals that this course was normally ineffective and that disorder only diminished when movement was made in the direction of the reforms which were needed.

In the short-term, it is difficult to be optimistic about public order in Britain. Ten years' ago, at the end of his study of urban disadvantage in the London Borough of Hackney, Harrison (1983, p. 435) came to a gloomy prognosis:

> The British system is not self-correcting. Thus the process of polarisation may continue in intensity. Unless its present course is quickly and radically reversed, Britain could become a country as deeply and destructively divided as many in Latin America. Revolution does not seem likely, rather a chaos of individual and sectional pathologies and disruptions ... Police methods will become the primary response to socio-economic grievances. As the threats

to law and order grow, so will the pressure for stricter measures to contain them, reducing the civil liberties of everyone.

It has been argued in this paper that in many British cities six trends are evident: growing ineffectiveness of government programmes, a decrease in levels of identity with the polity, falling opportunities for political participation, declining voluntary consent, diminishing perceptions of the regime's legitimacy and a growing experience of injustice. The conditions which have given rise to these factors are unemployment, social deprivation, political exclusion and powerlessness, alleged police malpractice and racial discrimination and disadvantage.

Lord Scarman, in 1981, came to the view that 'the riots were essentially an outburst of anger and resentment by young black people against the police', and he pointed to unemployment, urban deprivation, racial disadvantage and political exclusion as key factors leading to the unrest. These characteristics are common to all the areas in which serious urban unrest occurred in Britain during the 1980s. They result in frustrated expectations, cumulative disappointment and increasing resentment. These experiences lead to disenchantment with political procedures; they reduce identity with mainstream society and they undermine confidence in, and the legitimacy of, political institutions and rules; they increase perceptions of injustice; and they erode social controls and value consensus.

Unfortunately, there is little evidence that matters are likely to improve and the sombre outcome of the continued exclusion of these citizens may be an increased repudiation of political authority, a refusal to comply with laws and directives and increased conflict and violence. There is little evidence at present that British society and government are prepared to take real action against racism, urban disadvantage and social injustice.

The police will continue to have to deal with people, especially young people, with frustrated expectations, cumulative disappointment and increasing resentment. Inevitably, while the underlying conditions persist there remains a high potential in certain areas for conflict and for escalation into serious disorder.

Good government entails the maintenance of public order, stability and security for they provide the basis upon which prosperity, liberty and a high quality of life may develop. During the postwar period, the UK was widely seen as homogeneous, with relatively high levels of government legitimacy, common values, and public consent. Since 1980, however, crime and collective violence have risen alongside disadvantage and social division. In this respect, at least, the last 13 years in Britain have been a period of alarmingly bad government.

BIBLIOGRAPHY

Almond, G. and Verba, S. (1963) *The Civic Culture: Political Attitudes and Democracy in Five Nations*, New Jersey: Princeton University Press.

Bachrach, P. and Baratz, M. (1973) *Power and Poverty*, Oxford: Oxford University Press.

Banfield, E. (1968) 'Rioting mainly for fun and profit', in J. Q. Wilson (ed.), *The Metropolitan Enigma*, Cambridge, Mass.: Harvard University Press.

Benyon, J. (ed.), (1984) *Scarman and After: Essays Reflecting on Lord Scarman's Report, the Riots and their Aftermath*, Oxford: Pergamon Press.

Benyon, J. (1986) 'Spiral of decline: race and policing', in Z. Layton-Henry and P. Rich (eds.), *Race, Government and Politics in Britain*, London: MacMillan.

Benyon, J. and Bourn, C. (eds.) (1986) *The Police: Powers, Procedures and Proprieties*, Oxford: Pergamon Books.

Benyon, J. and Solomos, J. (eds.) (1987) *The Roots of Urban Unrest*, Oxford: Pergamon Press.

Binder, L. et al., (1971) *Crises and Sequences in Political Development*, New Jersey: Princeton University Press.

Brightmore, C. (1992) *Urban Rioting in Latter Day Britain*, dissertation submitted for MA in Public Order, University of Leicester (unpublished).

Brown, C. (1984) *Black and White Britain: The Third PSI Survey*, London: Heinemann.

Buss, A. (1961) *The Psychology of Aggression*, New York: Wiley.

Campbell, B. (1993) *Goliath: Britain's Dangerous Places*, London: Methuen

Carlyle, T. (1892) *Chartism*, London: Chapman and Hall.

Clutterbuck, R. (1980) *Britain in Agony*, Harmondsworth: Penguin.

Clutterbuck, R. (1983) *The Media and Political Violence*, London: Macmillan.

Cohen, S. (1973) *Folk Devils and Moral Panics*, St. Albans: Paladin.

Dahrendorf, R. (1980) 'Effectiveness and legitimacy: on the "governability" of democracies', *Political Quarterly*, Vol. 51, No. 4.

Davies, J. (1979) 'The J-curve of rising and declining satisfactions as a cause of revolution and rebellion', in H. Graham and T. Gurr (eds.) *Violence in America*, London: Sage.

Defoe, D. (1730) *An Effectual Scheme for the Immediate Prevention of Street Robberies and Suppressing of all other Disorders of the Night; with a Brief History of the Night-houses and an Appendix Relating to those Sons of Hell Call'd Incendiaries,* London, cited by A. Silver in D.J. Bordua (ed.), *The Police: Six Sociological Essays*, New York: John Wiley, 1967.

Dollard, J. *et. al.*, (1974) *Frustration and Aggression*, New Haven: Yale University Press.

Dunning, E., Murphy, P. and Williams, J. (1987) *The Social Roots of Football Hooligan Violence*, London: Routledge and Kegan Paul.

Field, S. (1982) 'Urban disorders in Britain and America', in S. Field and P. Southgate, *Public Disorder*, London: HMSO (HORPU Study No. 72).

Grew, R. (ed.), (1978) *Crises of Political Development in Europe and the United States*, New Jersey: Princeton University Press.

Gurr, T. (1968) 'A causal model of civil strife', *American Political Science Review*, Vol. 62, pp. 1104–1124.

Gurr, T. (1970) *Why Men Rebel*, New Jersey: Princeton University Press.

Halevy, E. (1912) *A History of the English People*, Vol. 1, New York.

Hall, S., Critcher, C., et al., (1978) *Policing the Crisis: Mugging, the State and Law and Order*, London: Macmillan, 1978.

Hall, S. and Jefferson, T. (eds.), (1976) *Resistance Through Rituals*, London: Hutchinson.

Hampton, C. (ed.) (1984) *A Radical Reader*, Harmondsworth: Penguin.

Harrison, P. (1983) *Inside the Inner City*, Harmondsworth: Penguin.

Hirschman, A.O. (1970) *Exit, Voice and Loyalty*, Cambridge, Mass.: Harvard University Press.

Hobsbawm, E.J. (1959) *Primitive Rebels*, Manchester: Manchester University Press.

Huntingdon, S. (1968) *Political Order in Changing Societies*, New Haven: Yale University Press.

Ingham, R. (ed.), (1978) *Football Hooliganism: the Wider Context*, London: Inter-Action Imprint.

Jenkinson, J. (1993) 'The 1919 riots' in P. Panyani (ed.) *Racial Violence in Britain, 1840–1950*, Leicester: Leicester University Press

Johnson, C. (1968) *Revolutionary Change*, London: University of London Press.

Keith, M. (1993) *Race, Riots and Policing*, London: UCL Press

Le Bon, G. (1960) *The Crowd*, New York: Viking Press.

Lowenthal, R. (1984) *Social Change and Cultural Crisis*, New York: Columbia University Press.

McCord, W. and Howard, J. (1968) 'Negro opinions in three riot cities', *American Behavioural Scientist*, Vol. 11, No. 4.

Millikan, M. and Blackmer, D. (eds.) (1961) *The Emerging Nations*, Boston: Little, Brown and Co.

Murdock, G. (1984) 'Reporting the riots: images and impact', in J. Benyon (ed.) *Scarman and After*, Oxford: Pergamon Press.

National Advisory Committee on Criminal Justice Standards and Goals (1976) *Disorders and Terrorism*, Washington: US Government.

Newman, Sir K. (1987) 'Will "no do" turn to "no go"?', *Police*, Vol. XIX, No. 7, March 1987.

Offe, C. (1984) *Contradictions of the Welfare State*, London: Hutchinson.

Pearson, G. (1983) *Hooligan!*, London: Macmillan.

Philips, Sir C. (1983) 'Politics in the making of the English police', in *The Home Office*, London: RIPA.

Reiner, R. (1985) *The Politics of the Police*, (2nd edition: 1992), Brighton: Wheatsheaf.

Rude, G. (1981) *The Crowd in History 1730–1848*, London: Lawrence and Wishart.

Scarman, L. (1981) *The Brixton Disorders 10–12 April 1981: Report of an Inquiry by the Rt. Hon the Lord Scarman*, OBE, London: HMSO, Nov. 1981 (Cmnd. 8427).

Sears, D. and McConahay, J. (1973) *The Politics of Violence: the New Urban Blacks and the Watts Riot*, Boston: Houghton Miflin.

Smith, D.J. (1983) *Police and People in London*, Vols. 1 and 4, London: Policy Studies Institute.

Spilerman, S. (1976) 'Structural characteristics of cities and the severity of racial disorders', *American Sociological Review*, Vol. 41, October 1976.

Stevenson, J. (1979) *Popular Disturbances in England 1700–1870*, London: Longman.

Thomas, K. (1978) 'The United Kingdom' in R. Grew (ed.), *Crises of Political Development in Europe and the United States*, New Jersey: Princeton University Press.

Thompson, E.P. (1968) *The Making of the English Working Class*, Harmondsworth: Penguin.

Thompson, E.P. (1971) 'The moral economy of the English crowd in the eighteenth century', *Past and Present*, Vol. 50, pp. 76-136.

Tullock, G. (1971) 'The paradox of revolution', *Public Choice*, Vol. 11, pp. 89–100.

Urwin, D. W. (1982) 'Territorial structures and political developments in the United Kingdom', in S. Rokkan and D.W. Urwin (eds.), *The Politics of Territorial Identity*, London: Sage.

Waddington, D. (1992) *Contemporary Issues in Public Disorder*, London: Routledge.

Waddington, D., Jones, K. and Critcher, C. (1989) *Flashpoints: Studies in Public Disorder*, London: Routledge.

THE AUTHOR

John Benyon is Professor of Politics and Director of the Centre for the Study of Public Order at the University of Leicester. He has written a number of books and articles on riots and collective violence, policing, inner-city politics, race relations and public disorder and the political agenda. His books include *Scarman and After* (1984: editor), *The Police* (1986: co-editor with Colin Bourne), *A Tale of Failure: Race and Policing* (1986) and *The Roots of Urban Unrest* (1987: co-editor with John Solomos). His recent research has included a study of social justice and order in the inner-cities, a study of African Caribbean People in Leicestershire and a project investigating police, crime and justice in Europe. John Benyon is currently Treasurer of the Political Studies Association, Editor of *Politics Review* and Editor of the series of books on *Contemporary Political Studies*, published by Harvester Wheatsheaf.

CENTRE FOR THE STUDY OF PUBLIC ORDER

UNIVERSITY OF LEICESTER

The Centre was established in 1987 to develop work in the fields of riots and disorder, policing, race relations and urban disadvantage. Research, teaching and professional training are undertaken in public disorder, criminology, policing, security management and information technology, and associated fields. The work is wide-ranging, taking 'public order issues' to include the study of how order is sustained in societies as well as considering how and in what circumstances order can be threatened or destroyed.

The Centre is interested in the nature, causes and consequences of disorder, such as riots, violent protest and terrorism, and also in mechanisms of social control. Other questions centre on how political and social institutions may affect order, and issues in crime prevention and security management.

Perceptions of Social Justice

The interests of the Centre thus extend from the study of riots and other public disorder, assessments of violence and crime and its prevention and detection, and examinations of policing policies and methods, to explorations of race relations and inner-city issues. The Centre is particularly interested in the political and social context and consequences of crime and disorder, the significance of perceptions of social justice, and the processes of social change.

Other topics of interest include social movements and political change; media coverage and its impact; technology and security; the changing nature of democracies; political participation; violence and the political agenda; civil liberties and citizenship.

Masters Programme

MA in Public Order: This degree explores political and social change, urban problems, race relations and the changing context in which modern policing takes place. It offers a comprehensive study of theories of collective violence, contemporary policing issues, the significance of social justice, riots, civil unrest and other forms of disorder, and ways whereby crime and disorder can be increased.

MA in Criminology: This degree offers a wide ranging, inter-disciplinary perspective on the extent, type and explanations of crime, together with an analysis of the criminal justice system, including police work, the courts, sentencing, imprisonment, and other forms of punishment and rehabilitation.

MSc in Security and Information Technology: This is a unique course which looks at the areas of risk and security management. It has three core courses: crime at work; management principles and capabilities; and research and technology in security management. As part of the course, students go on placement for 12 weeks with the security department of a major company.

The Centre's Approach

Emphasis is placed on collaboration with colleagues elsewhere in the world, and the Centre has particularly good links with experts in Europe, the United States and Asia. Funding for the Centre's work comes from a number of sources including the Joseph Rowntree Charitable Trust, the Economic and Social Research Council, the Home Office, the European Commission, private sector companies, local authorities, central government and the police service. In the last two years the Centre has received research funding of some £460,000 from external sources.

The Centre is multi-disciplinary in its methods and theories, and lays stress on historical and comparative approaches and on the importance of political and social theory. The Centre seeks to promote an enlightened approach to public order issues, and puts the pursuit of social justice as a primary goal.